GOOGLE CLASSROOM 2021:

A useful, updated guide for teachers and students using distance learning; including 7 working tricks for optimizing management and productivity!

Table of Contents

Introduction

G oogle Classroom is a free online tool enabling teachers and students to freely exchange files among themselves. Teachers will post homework for the pupils, often without needing to print out. This also acts as a way to connect. Teachers are required to post ads and future tasks, as well as contact all students and guardians.

Teachers will find that it makes their teaching more effective with all the options and can save them a lot of time. If we could give something to teachers that would save them time, save the money from teaching, interact more with students and parents, support struggling with learners, and improve students' learning environment, will they consider using it? We hope they will.

For teachers and students, it will save them time, effort, paper, and it will allow teachers to create a better environment for assignments and quizzes, and you can always talk to parents and guardians with this. You can copy and tweak assignments as well one to another, and control multiple classes as well, which is great if you are looking to truly master this type of system. It is great for students and teachers alike and allows for a collaborative system that will in turn create a better and more immersive system than you have thought possible.

Google Classroom is also increasing student engagements and keeping them motivated by allowing teachers to motivate them in plenty of ways. Likewise, it gives them the latest information and trends. Web-based contents and materials are also accessible to them. Classrooms all around the world can soon be connected and that will broaden information.

For educators, Google Classroom makes it easier for them to deliver instructions while keeping their lessons, student-centered. Now they have more time for discussions and answering questions or conducting problem-solving instead of doing and checking homework. Students also have an adequate amount of time to understand the subjects.

Immediate assistance from the teacher is a must for students to continually grow and Google Classroom only enhances this aspect. This helps teachers to build and store assignments using Google Forms, Google Docs, and several other resources provided by Google.

Let's get started with this wonderful online classroom technology!

CHAPTER 1:

Distance Learning with Google Classroom

Y ou will need to be certain you're logged in to your Google account before you use Google Classroom. If you don't have one, you can use this book to build a Google account to get going or get guidance. You can navigate Google Classroom at classroom.google.com

LEARNING INNOVATION

Innovation is important at all levels of education, but teachers cannot understand the many technical tools available. Google Classroom is a free tool that is attracting recently.

The main purpose of this part is to evaluate whether teachers recognize the use of Google Classroom. This research was conducted with a subjective research plan. An example of a semi-structured meeting technology study involves 12 service teachers who have used Google Classroom in the classroom for at least a semester. The information obtained is obtained through extensive research, coding, and classification of information via Vivo Results that are displayed by the teacher only as a tool that can be used for classroom enrollment and basic management without significantly affecting the education program. Teacher responses suggest that there is no easy-to-understand interface behind efficiency. Additional tests can be guided by students' perspectives.

PROBLEM STATEMENT

To improve class efficiency, teachers aim to increase student engagement by making student experiences more personalized and independent, while multiple schools, universities, and higher education institutions work in mixed learning periods to create (Spring, Haddock and Graham, 2016). Google Classroom can be used as a mixed learning tool to improve classroom profitability. The lack of searches in Google's classrooms, particularly for developing countries, has highlighted the potential of this tool to be explored further. The use of appropriate technology is perhaps the biggest test for teachers to face in a mixed learning environment; therefore, this research focuses on evaluating the feasibility of Google lessons in universities.

CHAPTER 2:

How To Use This Innovation To Conduct Classes

GETTING STARTED

The first thing you need to do when you open Google Classroom is to develop a lesson. At the top-right corner, press the Plus button, and then pick 'Create' class. This will pull up a dialog box asking whether you want to use Google Classroom for students at a university.

Google Classroom allows schools to use G Suite for Learning. This offers additional protection and protective safeguards for teachers and pupils. When you use Google Classroom for your personal use, there's no reason to think about that. You will then have to enter your class name. If you are using a Classroom in a school and still want to include the details, there's also the method to enter a Subject, Section, and Room. Once finished, click Create. When you have built a profile, you are going to be brought to the page of that profile.

You'll need to add your students to that until you've built your lesson. Inviting students via email is one way you can do it. To do this, you'll have to navigate to the People tab first. Tap the Invite button for Students. It will bring up the menu where you can type different email addresses of your students. Once those have been added, click Invite. It will give your students an update, with a connection welcoming them to enter your classroom online. The second choice to connect students to the class is to use a certificate for the class. It is a shortcode and can be used by others to enter the class if you give it to them. First, press on the Category Preferences icon in the top-right corner to use it. You can find the code for the class under the heading General. You can exchange the class code with the students after that, as you wish.

USING CLASSROOM ON MOBILE

The Google classroom web service is available for mobile devices including Android and iOS.

This is helpful because you will be able to access and create classes with just your Smartphone.

Because a Smartphone can be taken anywhere with you, it is a nice way to have access to your class without needing to carry a bulky laptop bag around.

One of the advantages of using Google classroom for your online learning and teacher to student collaboration is that it runs on mobile devices.

To get started with using Google classroom on your mobile device, you will need to have the application installed on your Android or iOS phone. The mobile application helps you to organize and manage your classroom wherever you are without needing your laptop.

That means you get all the functionalities that are available in the Google classroom web service right in your mobile phone without needing to open a web browser such as Chrome to assess your classroom.

The mobile app has similar features and user interfaces with the Chrome Web app. Meaning you can run everything that you do with the Chrome Web App using a mobile phone.

CREATE AN ASSIGNMENT (PART 1)

Within Google Classroom assignments can be created and assigned to students, and there are a variety of useful choices for educators here. Here's what you got to know:

- Open the class you wish to apply a job to

- At the top of the list, click the tab Classwork

- Click the Create button and pick to add a task

- Offer your assignment a title and include any more directions or explanations in the box below

- Click on the date to select your assignment date and add time if you want to decide when it is due on a specified day

- By clicking on one of the icons next to the word Assign, choose the type of assignment you want to create. Your choices include uploading a file from your computer, inserting a Google Drive file, adding a YouTube video, or adding a link to a website.

- Press Assign to send your students the assignment.

If you want to give more than one class the same assignment, click on the class name in the top-left corner of the assignment window and pick all the classes you want to add to it.

CREATE AN ASSIGNMENT (PART 2)

However, selecting a Drive tool in Google Classroom has an added value, and this becomes obvious with the choices you get when selecting a file from the Drive.

1. Students may view the file: If you want all students to be able to access the file, choose this option but not be able to change it in any way. This is perfect for study guides and standardized handouts to which the entire class must have access.

2. Students can edit the file: If you want all students to be able to edit and work on the same paper, choose this. This would be perfect for a collaborative learning project where students in the same Google Presentation that work on different slides, or where they are collaboratively brainstorming ideas about something you want to discuss in your next learning.

3. Make a copy for each student: If you choose this option, the Classroom will make every student in your class a copy of the original file and grant them editing rights to that file. The master of the instructor shall remain intact and the students shall have no access to the original register. Choose that if you want a paper that has an essay question for students to work on easily, or a digital worksheet prototype where students fill in the blanks with their answers. This level of automation was possible before Google Classroom but when incorporated into this new platform, it is much easier to handle.

ORGANIZE ASSIGNMENTS BY TOPIC

A recent change to Google Classroom is its ability to organize topic-by-theme assignments. This helps you to group assignments together in the Classwork tab, by unit or form. Students and teachers will consider the task they are searching for more effectively.

Follow the instructions below to create Topics.

- Navigate to your class

- Click on the tab Classwork

- Click on the button "Create"

- Select "Topic"

- Name your topic and "Add"

You can add new assignments to a topic from the creation screen for the assignment. Simply click the drop-down box next to the Subject before allocating it.

If you have already generated assignments that need to be transferred to a topic, follow these steps:

- Click on the Classwork tab

- Hover over the assignment you want to move with your mouse

- Click the three dots

- Choose Edit

- Look for the drop-down box next to Topic

- Click the drop-down and choose the Topic you want to move it to

How students complete their assignments & send them

A more convenient approach, however, is to press the menu button in the screen's top left-hand corner and pick To-do from the pop-out display. Clicking on one of those assignments will open the student's related tab. If it is a Google Drive file, in the top right-hand corner, next to the Sharing button, an additional button is attached to the toolbar. This button has the "Turn it in" label. Clicking on it submits to the instructor their assignment.

GRADING AND RETURNING ASSIGNMENTS TO STUDENTS

Teachers will consider a variety of different ways to search for pupils. Perhaps the most effective method, however, is to join the class that you are involved in grading and clicking from the Stream view on the assigned name.

- Look at the sidebar at the top left of the Stream view and you will see the "Coming Assignments" box if you notice that assignments get lost between student conversations. Tap on the assignment to be evaluated, and obey the instructions below:

- Click on the name of the student who submitted an assignment you would like to rate.

- Use the commenting features in Drive to leave comprehensive feedback on particular parts of the student submission when the document opens. When you're done, shut down the folder. All modifications are automatically saved.

- Click on the right of the name of the student when you return to Classroom where it says, "No grade" and enter a point-based grade for the assignment.

- Check the box next to the student you have just graded, then click the "Return" button to save the grade and inform the student that their paper has been graded

- Add any additional input in the pop-up box, then click on "Return Assignment"

GRADING TIPS AND MORE INFORMATION

How do the students think I was grading their assignment? Am I needed to rate an assignment out of 100? These and more questions will be answered below.

- When a teacher returns a student's assignment, the teacher no longer has the right to edit the text.

- You can return a student's assignment without marking it by simply checking the box next to the name of the student and pressing Return. That may be useful for error-submitted assignments.

- When returning an assignment to a student they will immediately receive an email message reminding them of your actions

- You can change a grade at any time by clicking on the grade and then clicking "Edit."

- It is useful for a one-time analysis of all the assignments submitted.

- The default number of points for an assignment is 100, but by clicking the drop-down arrow and selecting another value, typing your value, or even choosing the option not to score an assignment, you can adjust that.

Are you ready to dig deeper into Google Classroom? If so, follow the instructions and screenshots step-by-step to make them easy to follow and apply.

CHAPTER 3:

How To Create And Join Classes

HOW SETUP STEP BY STEP CLASSROOM CORRECTLY

Follow these means to set up your Google Classroom:

Go to: classroom.google.com.

•Google Classroom is currently accessible for Google for Education accounts just as standard Gmail accounts. Anybody with a Google record would now be able to utilize Google Classroom.

Snap-on the "+" button in the upper option to make your five stars.

(It's close to the checkerboard symbol you use to get to the entirety of your applications.) Then snap "Make class."

•If you're beginning just because your screen will probably resemble the one above.

•If you have a few classes as of now, they'll show on this home screen. You can include new courses with the "+" button.

Include data about your group.

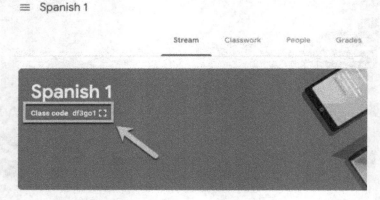

•The "subject" field lets you browse a rundown of class subjects or type your own. (This field is discretionary.)

When your class is made, students can begin going along with it.

•Students can get your class together with a join code (above). This is a brisk, straightforward approach to get students into your group. By showing the join code, students can sign in to Google Classroom, click the "+" catch, and "Join class" to enter the join code. At that point, they're added to your group.

•You can welcome students to your group by email. This is a decent alternative if students don't meet face to face for your group. To do this, click the "Individuals" tab at the top. At that point, click the "Welcome Students" button (a symbol with an individual and an or more). You can welcome students separately with email addresses or by gatherings if all students are in a Google Group.

CUSTOMIZE YOUR GOOGLE CLASSROOM

•There won't be any students in your group the second you make it. This is an ideal opportunity to get innovative and have some good times with it! Snap "Select subject" on the right side of the header. It will open an exhibition of header pictures you can use to flavor up your study hall.

Communicate with your class here

You can likewise transfer a photograph to show at the highest point of your Classroom. You can utilize a picture of your group or something that relates to your group. A few instructors will make a custom header picture with essential data and fun designs. Utilize this layout to create a header.

INSTRUCTIONS TO UTILIZE CLASSROOM IN A REGULAR CLASS

After your group is set up and students go along with, you have a completely working Google Classroom platform. Congrats!

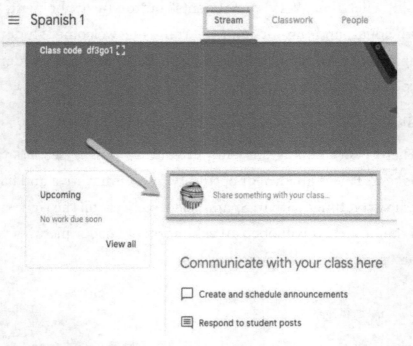

Be that as it may, you would prefer not to stop there. Here are a few things you can do in your Classroom:

INCLUDE AN ANNOUNCEMENT

This is a decent method to speak with your group and give them information. Declarations are presented on the class stream, yet there isn't an evaluation related to them.

Go to your group Stream and snap on "share something with your group."

Include the content for your declaration. Include any documents (joined or from Google Drive), YouTube recordings, or connections you'd like. At that point, post it (or schedule it for some other time).

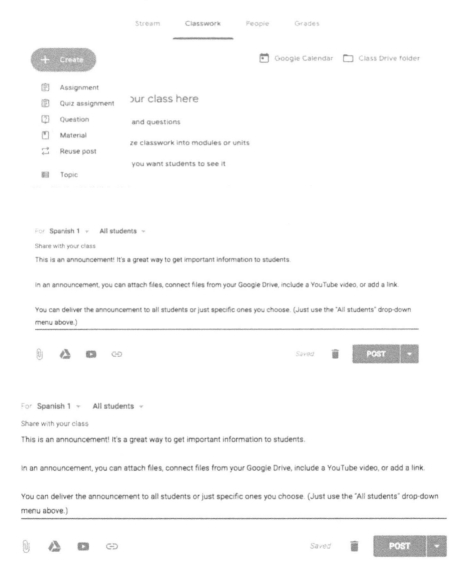

Make a task, test, question, joining material, or reuse an old post

Things to remember for your task or question:

•Elucidating title for your task. (Expert tip: It's acceptable to number your assignments to dispense with disarray.)

•A portrayal. This is useful for students who were missing and for alluding back to a past task later.

•Points. Pick what number of focuses the task/question is worth (or utilize the drop-down menu to make it ungraded).

•A due date. Pick when the task is expected (or don't utilize a due date).

•A point. (We'll get to this in a second ...)

•File connections. Append records, including documents from Google Drive, incorporate YouTube recordings, or give students a link.

Allocate the task quickly, plan it to post naturally later, or spare your task as a draft to complete then.

Arrange your class with points

And when you have various parts, units, subjects, and so on inside your group, you can arrange your assignments and inquiries by the theme to keep everything sorted out.

Under "Classwork," click the "Make" catch and include a point. At that point, at whatever point you make another task or declaration, you'll have the option to add that subject to it.

EVALUATION AND BRING WORK BACK

When students have finished work, you can give criticism and grade the task. Snap-on the "Classwork" catches and snap on the task to see student work.

Here is a portion of the moves you can make ...

1. Sort the task by students who have handed the work over or all students who were given the job. (Simply click on the vast number.) Or, you can sort by different alternatives with the drop-down menu underneath the immense amounts.)

2. Open and see student work by tapping on it. Inside student records, slide introductions, and so on., you can add remarks straightforwardly to the document. Or on the other hand ...

3. Type and see private remarks to the student by tapping on the student's name. You can likewise observe when documents were turned in with history.

4. Add an evaluation to student work.

5. When you're entirely done, return work to students. Be sure you've checked the crate close to their names and snap the "Arrival" button.

STEP BY STEP INSTRUCTIONS TO CREATE A CLASS

Fortunately, this is anything but difficult to do. Here's the ticket.

1. Navigate to https://classroom.google.com
2. Choose the "I am a Teacher" alternative

3. Click the "+" sign in the upper right-hand corner close to your Google account
4. Select "Make Class," at that point, give it a name and a segment, and snap "Make."

The "Segment" field is an optional descriptor for your group, so here you might need to include something like the first period, evaluation level, or some other short portrayal.

CUSTOMIZE THE APPEARANCE OF YOUR CLASS

From the moment you make the class, we will have the possibility to insert a default header image. This is the image that students will see when they click on your group to get to their homework and statements.

You can edit this image with a couple of quick steps.

1. Hover your mouse over the pennant picture
2. Look for the Select Theme connect in the base right-hand corner
3. Click Select Theme to open a display of photographs you can decide for your group.
4. Choose a picture from the display. At that point, click Select Class Theme to change your header picture.

There is an assortment of pictures to look over, yet most are themed on a scholarly subject.

STEP BY STEP INSTRUCTIONS TO ADD STUDENTS TO GOOGLE CLASSROOM

HOMEROOM COMMUNICATION

There are two different ways to empower discourse among students and educators in Google Classroom. The first is the Stream - a Facebook-like mass of messages that can be seen by all individuals of the class. This element is accessible to the two students and instructors.

The following method to convey is by utilizing email. Students can tap the three dabs close to their educator's name on the class landing page to open a Gmail message that is auto-filled with their teacher's email address. Students can likewise email each other by tapping the Students tab and tapping on the three spots to one side of the student's name and choosing Email Student.

Educators can do a similar thing when they click on the "Individuals" tab, be that as it may, they have the extra choice of choosing different students and afterward clicking Actions > Email to make an impression on a gathering of students.

ADDING YOUR STUDENTS TO THE COURSE

When you have made all the classes that you need, you can rapidly add students to your program. This should be possible in two different ways. The first is to have students register themselves.

Note that the class code can be changed or crippled whenever by the educator. Click the drop-down close to the class code and decide to reset or disable it as you feel the need. Resetting or impairing the code won't influence students who have just enlisted for your group.

The following method to include students is for the instructor to add them physically. This is moderately clear and maybe not as monotonous as you would suspect. Here's how it works.

1. Click on the class that you need to add students to
2. Then snap the "Individuals" tab at the highest point of the page
3. Click the Invite Students symbol (an or more sign close to an individual)
4. A pursuit box will show up permitting you to scan for the email locations of individual students, contact gatherings, or Google Groups.

Note that instructors utilizing G Suite for Education can just include students who are a piece of their Google space. If your students are using open Gmail accounts, they won't have the option to get to your online substance in Google Classroom. This is purposeful and is a piece of the security and protection that Google needs to guarantee instructors and students have when utilizing this stage.

CHAPTER 4:

Privacy Settings For Teachers And Students

Google Classroom is completely coordinated with the Google ecosystem. There are some third-party add-ons that you can try, here are a couple of valuable ones:

- *Hiver*: with Google Classroom and Gmail sharing a symbiotic relationship, your inbox can end up overflowing. Hiver will allow teachers to keep their

Gmail inbox sorted out and team up with partners and school services without any problem.

- *Effectively Learn*: this device is planned for improving the reading skills of students. Its addition permits educators to import Classroom lists to Learn Actively. Like this, you can centralize where you share your reading assignments.

- *GeoGebra Classic*: this tool helps students with making numerical models, diagrams, spreadsheets, and so on. GeoGebra Classic integration allows teachers to use application materials as assignments to their Google Classroom..

- There are a lot more Google Classroom integrations and G Suite additional items that you can try out.

SECURITY AND BACKUP

Here is a portion of the major highlights in regards to Google Classroom's security, protection, and backup features:

- Google Classroom is secured under the center G Suite for Education Terms of Service, which is agreeable with the Family Educational Rights and Privacy Act of 1974

- Third-party applications can get to Classroom information just if admins give the authorization to do as such

- Google claims that they never utilize your content or student data for advertising purposes
- G Suite for Education also allows schools to choose which Google services their students can use
- Google gives schools free and unlimited storage on Google Drive

How would you find support?

You can contact Google's 24/7 helpline or visit their online help center.

PRICING

Google Classroom is free for all the schools that are utilizing G Suite for Education. However, some Google Classroom integrations and add-ons may come at an extra expense.

CHEATS AND SECRETS

Ways to Prevent Fraud in Your Google Form Quiz

Google Forms is an excellent tool for organizing and automating digital tests. Here are some tips for the "fraudulent" design of Google forms!

If you use Google modules to run tests and quizzes in your class, you probably know that some students have found different ways to "play" the modules to get a better grade:

1. Open a tab to search for answers

2. Preview the module before the lesson to find the answers

3. Send questions to your friends

4. Share answers with friends

5. Take screenshots of quiz questions

6. View the HTML page root for answers

7. Look at a friend's screen to choose the answers

8. Right-click the words to check the definitions and spelling

9. Share answers with classmates over time

10. Write "Cheats" on your hand or card

This should not be shocking that students are searching for ways to boost their test scores. (You could have been that student when you were in school !!)

I believe formative and summative assessments play an appropriate role in the classroom.

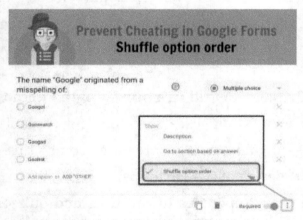

Mixing the answer options makes it more difficult for "Screen Creepers" to copy a classmate's answers.

Note: Google Forms has a "Mix order of questions" feature. However, using this feature can cause problems. I recommend mixing the answers to the questions.

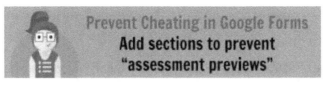

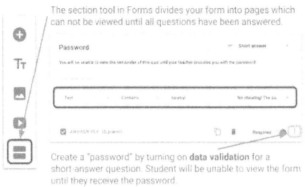

The section tool in Forms divides your form into pages which can not be viewed until all questions have been answered.

Password · Short answer

You will be unable to view the remainder of this quiz until your teacher provides you with the password

| Text | Contains | receive | No cheating! The pa... |

ANSWER KEY (0 points) Required

Create a "password" by turning on **data validation** for a short-answer question. Student will be unable to view the form until they receive the password.

Use page sections to block assessment previews.

Add parts to your quiz, so students don't preview a pre-class form.

If you post your questionnaire from Google Classroom early in the day, this is a growing issue.

A "password" to prevent students from proceeding until you are ready will go a step further.

 You can even insert your code.

You can conveniently collect your personal information (name/section) on the first page. But before you access the query, a password is needed.

Set your password by inserting a prompt response and asking for a particular number or phrase with the data verification feature.

Note: This approach is not 100 % safe and should not be used to encrypt sensitive information.

To build alternate assessment paths using page breaks.

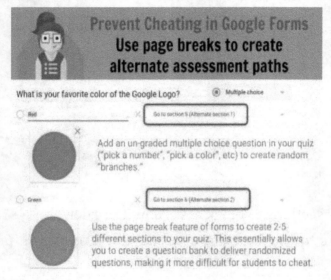

The questionnaire feature of Google Forms cannot be used for each student to construct specific evaluations.

However, by creating a branched form, you can build a similar experience.

Next, add to your quiz a question of multiple unrated choices: "Choose a number," "Choose a color," etc.

Then, set 3-5 separate quiz sections using the feature above in Tip 2. Attach as many questions to each section as you want.

Finally, add a "Go-To" rule to direct students to another section of them based on their answer to the unmarked question you added.

PREVENTING FRAUD BY ASKING BETTER QUESTIONS!

•Sequence questions: Use the "checkbox" question type to ask students to sequence or arrange items in a list.

•Corresponding questions: use the multiple-choice grid question type to create a corresponding question (ideal for vocabulary tests!)

•Reading pass: use the title/text element to add a short reading pass.

•Video question: ask students to watch a video and then answer the questions (ideal for math and the world's language).

•Photo question: photos should be used as a resource or as a choice of questions (ideal for scientific, mathematical, social, and primary school students).

•Free answer/short answer - If a student can correctly answer all multiple-choice questions, but cannot formulate 2-3 sentences on the same topic, there is something wrong.

On or via Google Classroom, you can activate this feature on the settings page of the Google app.

Using some / all of the suggestions listed above, you have done your part to protect the integrity of your reviews and encourage your students to practice academic honesty.

This is not realistic to be 100 % confident that students cannot trick an assessment. In the end, they damage themselves and their academic growth. Our job is to encourage them, educate them, and train them, do their best, and show good character, even if they have the opportunity to cheat.

CHAPTER 5:

Advantages And Drawbacks Of Classroom

W ouldn't you like to use a platform that enables you to interact with students and provide them with constructive feedback within the classroom? Google Classroom does just this as it represents Google's groundbreaking introduction into the world of online education within the LMS sector and it has been designed to make classrooms worldwide not just paperless but also more efficient. Google Classroom is accessible through Google Apps for Training since it is primarily designed for educational institutions and not for corporate management.

ADVANTAGES OF GOOGLE CLASSROOM

EASILY ACCESSIBLE AND SIMPLE TO USE

Even if you don't use Google regularly, using Google Classroom is still pretty easy. Aside from being accessible through the Chrome application, it is generally available on most laptops, cell phones, and tablets. This enables people to use Google Docs, upload YouTube videos, or insert links and download files through Google Drive. Moreover, users will find it completely simple to log into Google classroom to start receiving and completing certain tasks.

EFFECTIVE SHARING AND COMMUNICATION SYSTEM

One of Google Classroom's most useful apps is Google Docs as such files are saved electronically and can be shared with an unlimited number of people. Moreover, if you update a document or task through Google Docs, students can access such files directly from their Google Drive, as long as they have been shared with them. Instructors also no longer need to send files individually to each student via email as sharing one file link with them is sufficient.

EFFICIENT ASSIGNMENT SYSTEM

The fact that tasks can be completed and submitted with only the click of a button also makes Google Classroom particularly useful to instructors. Surveying completed assignments has never been easier because you can quickly search through

Google Classroom to check and see who submitted their assignment versus those who are still working on it.

EFFICIENT FEEDBACK SYSTEM

In terms of input, Google Classroom offers you the ability to provide learners with immediate online help through reviews and comments provided by instructors.

GOING DIGITAL

If there ever comes a day when marking papers physically will no longer be needed, Google Classroom will surely facilitate this process. By compiling eLearning resources into one cloud space, instructors can go paperless and avoid the need to print and hand out assignments or notes to their students.

EASY TO USE AND CLEAN INTERFACE

Google Classroom also has a clean interface that makes individual interaction with the software easy and effective. In other words, internet users should feel pretty comfortable using the platform.

BEST DISCUSSION SYSTEM

For a wide range of online classes, learners can discuss specific matters and share URLs during their conversations online.

GOOGLE CLASSROOM FOR EVERYONE

Teachers can also access Google Classroom alongside guests, which ensures that you and your peers can create a Google

Classroom that can be used to host staff meetings, exchange knowledge, and discuss career growth.

DISADVANTAGES OF GOOGLE CLASSROOM

ACCOUNT MANAGING ISSUES

Google Classroom also doesn't require multi-domain exposure. You can't sign in to access your personal Gmail as you must log in to Google Apps to do so. As a result, if you already have a specific Google ID, it can be annoying to manage several Google Accounts. For instance, if you have a document or a picture in your Gmail that you would like to share through Google Classroom, you must save it individually on the hard drive of your device, sign out and then sign in with the Google Classroom profile once again.

GOOGLE EVERYWHERE

Google users may feel lost the first time they use Google Classroom because there are many keys with icons that are only known to Google users. In fact, despite greater collaboration between Google and YouTube, which helps stream videos, support for other platforms is not built-in. This can make it frustrating, for example, when you need to translate a Word document to a text document to use it. In general, your familiarity with Google influences your ability to use the Google Classroom setting easily.

AUTOMATED UPDATE ISN'T AVAILABLE

Since tasks do not always update immediately, students may have to refresh the server to ensure that they did not miss any important notifications.

Difficult Sharing Among Students

Students cannot share their research with their classmates unless they are the "owners" of a document.

This can also be troublesome as they may have to accept sharing alternatives, which would confuse if they were to share their work with a lot of their peers.

EDITING ISSUES

Once you create an assignment and send it to pupils, students become the "owners" and are therefore authorized to modify it. This can be problematic and misleading if students intentionally or accidentally erase certain sentences in the document.

AUTOMATED TESTS AND QUIZZES ARE NOT AVAILABLE

One feature that is not provided by Google Classroom is that it does not supply learners with standardized quizzes and assessments.

Hence, Google Classroom seems to be better suited to be used as part of a mixed learning environment rather than a purely online curriculum.

NO WEB CHAT

Google Classroom has not incorporated Google Hangouts, which poses a challenge when it comes to creating a mixed learning environment as online communication between teachers and students is only available via Google Docs. Since good communication necessitates engagement between students, the easiest way to do this is through online conversations, which remains currently unavailable via Google Classroom.

CHAPTER 6:

How To Use Classroom For Students

Teachers and educators can get quite a bit out of Google Classroom to organize their students and make their teaching more effective. They are allowed to monitor all of their students in one area, keeping classes separate, making announcements, and doing so much more to help students learn so they can spend more time teaching rather than spending so much time on their regular administrative tasks.

Students can also benefit from Google Classroom. While the students will not be able to add people to the class and are limited on the resources they can upload onto the platform, there are plenty of opportunities for them to interact with each other, communicate with the teacher, and learn in new ways!

LOGGING IN

At the beginning of the school year, your teacher will be able to invite you to join their classroom. You will simply need to give them a preferred email and then accept the invitation and link that they send to you later on. This will allow you access to the classroom, and you can see all the announcements and assignments that the teacher gives for that year. You can also stream content, read materials, take tests and quizzes, partake in discussions, and hand in homework assignments all in one place.

Make sure that the email address you provide is one you use often. Otherwise, you could miss out on some of the critical information needed to do well in class. Consider signing up for a Gmail account that is only for school and giving that to each teacher who uses Google Classroom. This allows all your school announcements to be in one place and limits the chance that something gets lost in another email address.

SHARING

Students are allowed to share their thoughts and opinions in the Classroom. Going to the Stream tab, you can provide an answer to discussion questions the teacher posts, and the whole class will be able to see. You can attach supporting documents to this as well including videos, weblinks, files, and documents.

This is separate from where you would do tests or essays and other homework. The Stream tab is a place where others will be able to see your information, what you have posted, and can even comment on it themselves. If you are doing a discussion question or you have found something interesting to share with the whole class, this is the option for you. If you are sending in a homework assignment or a test, you will use Google Forms or Drive to get this done.

ASSIGNMENTS

Your teacher will be able to upload assignments on Classroom for everyone to see. Rather than printing off papers and expecting a student to remember each task from multiple classes each day, Classroom allows the student to get into their class and find all the information needed for the assignment. To see your tasks, you simply need to click on the button to "View All" and see a list of assignments for a particular class. You can see To-Do items, such as if you need to read a document before starting, or a reminder for a test and students have the option to mark whether an assignment is done.

Many assignments will require a link or file to complete. For example, if a student needed to write out an essay or submit answers to a discussion question, they may have written the answers in Word outside of the Classroom. In these cases, the assignment feature allows students to upload these links. Students can also comment on an assignment but remember that others in the class will be able to see these comments.

If a student has a question about an assignment, they can simply email the teacher through their Gmail account. The teacher can then respond personally to the student, without notifying the whole class, and get the questions answered promptly.

ORGANIZATION

The classroom is hooked up to Google Calendar so students can look at their assignments, test dates, and other important information and find out when everything is due at a glance. This can help students to keep track of their jobs and makes it easier to plan out how to get all the work done. In Calendar, students can change the color to match with the class, and they can set up text message alerts to remind them of upcoming due dates on assignments.

FEEDBACK

Google Classroom allows students to discuss various parts of their homework and tests with the teacher. In a regular classroom setting, the student will submit the work, the teacher will grade it with a few comments, and that is the end. There isn't enough time in class for the student to discuss the grade or comment and many may not be able to bring up this discussion later. With Classroom, the student can leave a comment under feedback from the teacher, and a discussion can begin that helps the student understand why they got a particular grade or even clarify their answers. This allows for more analysis and learning than what may go on in the traditional classroom.

DISCUSSION TIME

Many teachers like the feature of adding discussion questions inside Classroom. These discussion questions allow students to talk about a particular topic and learn together in a setting that is more comfortable than speaking in the classroom. Sometimes the teacher may not have time for a full discussion in class and other times; this is a tool used to bring shy students out to speak their opinions. Either way, students are learning from each other, considering different ideas, and gaining more knowledge naturally.

GOOGLE APPS

Google has many great apps to use, and all of them are free. This makes it easy for students to get on and use everything that is needed on the platform. Through Google Classroom, students can enjoy other apps including Google Calendar, Google Spreadsheets, Docs, Presentation, Gmail, Drive, and much more. These are great tools that can help students out at any level of education, even if their class is not using Classroom at the time. Students will become familiar with using these apps on the platform and seeing what a difference they make in learning and presenting themselves.

OTHER FUNCTIONS AND BENEFITS OF CLASSROOM

There are so many great benefits to students using Google Classroom. While many times the focus is on the teacher and how they will be able to streamline their teaching process and help students learn more, students are getting some of the best benefits out of this tool. They are opening up to new ideas, finding creative ways to learn, and even having more teacher attention than in a traditional classroom. Some of the other benefits that students can enjoy using the Classroom include:

- If a particular lesson is not clear to the student, they can add feedback and save the lesson to a new folder for revisions later once clarification is met.

- Students can privately ask their teacher a question

- The ability to create and also monitor how they are doing in a particular class using Google Sheets.

- Ability to email either individual students or a group of students and start up a conversation. This can be helpful in discussions when missing a day in school, or for a project.

- Students can submit their assignments as attachments in many forms including links, videos, files, and voice clips.

- Reduce how much paper is used in the classroom.

- Fewer missed due dates since they have all their homework in one place and can monitor on Google Calendar at a glance.

- Shy students can reply to questions online and engage without being worried about talking in front of other people. This allows for more engagement out of the class and for everyone to be heard.

- The classroom is flexible, easy to access, and both instructors and students can receive benefits of using it.

- While Classroom is only available for students who attend an educational institution using the platform, all of the Google apps are available to everyone for free, allowing students and individuals to get the benefits of these apps, even if they aren't in class.

- Students can use Google Classroom on their smartphones, making it easier to receive notifications and work on assignments anywhere.

- It is easy for students to work together, even outside of class, and for teachers to provide feedback and comments on assignments so students learn more than ever.

- Better organization—students can keep all the information for one class in one place. This limits the likelihood of losing an assignment, forgetting about it, or leaving the paper at home. Students can simply log on to their classroom and complete homework assignments, tests, and more in one location.

- Instant feedback—taking tests can be hard, but it is nice to get immediate feedback. Your teacher can choose an add-on that provides instant feedback on test scores and some types of homework, allowing you a chance to see how you did right away rather than waiting a week or more for the teacher to have time to grade all the papers.

Google Classroom is a great learning companion for students. There are many great (and free!) apps that students may already know how to use. It facilitates different types of learning, allows even the quietest student in the class to speak up and be heard, and can help provide instant feedback and more discussion between students and teachers to help the student learn more than they can in a traditional classroom.

While teachers may love how Classroom helps them to be more effective at their jobs, students will enjoy how easy it makes the learning process and all the options it opens up in the class.

CHAPTER 7:

How To Organize Homework And Lessons For Teachers

BEST STRATEGIES AND TECHNIQUES

S trengthen your efficiency by following the classroom strategies written below:

GOOGLE CLASSROOM TECHNIQUES TO USE NOW

Google Classroom currently doesn't require teachers to cover assignments that have already been uploaded. This makes some sense when you think about all the ways a single assignment posted in the classroom embeds itself through Google Drive and Calendar on the side about stuff Google does.

But for teachers, that can be a painful problem. Pick the situation up.

Let's say that the night before my English class, I posted a stunning short story practice. The text is attached in the form of of.pdf.

That took at least five minutes — maybe more — to bring all of those tools together and post them as an assigned task.

But instead, the day occurs, and we don't get to the thing that is being prepared. There's something else that gets in the way, and we never get a chance to get into it.

ENABLE REAL-TIME FEEDBACK FOR PRESENTATIONS

Do a major favor to yourself and your learners by copying and pasting test models into any private statement before presentations.

Include spaces for an overall evaluation, success criteria, and emoji stars and wishes, etc. with spaces for each student in your class to get feedback. With all this put in place before student presentations, I can provide real-time, accurate, and informative feedback to students — whilst they are present. It means I don't assess their presentations after school, and they don't wait for feedback.

USE EMOJI TO CODE LEARNING ACTIVITIES

Begin each unit title and assign a name with an emoji theme, And send completed units and assignments an emoji checkmark to indicate in a glance they are behind us.

Include learning targets in every posted activity or assignment That's not as much a convenience event as it's great pedagogy. It will often send you back to the unit plan or the standard curricular, keeping you grounded. And reminding the students what the goal of each learning activity is will always be present. "Why should we do this?"

SHARE HOMEROOM CLASSES WITH ALL SPECIALIST STAFF

Let your language teachers, art teachers, and band teachers remove announcements and tools from your classroom. But if they don't, a great alternative is having access to your classroom.

POST ONCE TO MULTIPLE CLASSROOMS

Take advantage of the feature if you are a professional instructor. You don't have to post different assignments in every classroom. All relevant Classrooms are posted at once.

Adjust Google Classroom notifications to silence Classroom emails and notifications, which are not yours.

This strategy becomes relevant after discussing the two previous strategies about discussing Google Classroom. Switch off Classroom Notifications you don't teach.

They are not going to do it on their own, and we can't expect them to. Each week we have to set aside 15 minutes or more to ensure this life ability is happening.

Some would say email is not going to be around forever, and maybe they are right. But for the last 25 years, it has been working well, and it will not be going anywhere anytime soon. Ensure sure the students are learning how to maximize the inbox.

CREATE A SCHOOL-WIDE GOOGLE CLASSROOM

This allows for school-wide polls, debates, hot lunch order form submissions, yearbook photo submissions for the student, announcements delivery, etc. Full disclosure: I am not currently using this — partly in an attempt to slow down the flow of ideas I'm pushing on colleagues in a new teaching community. But at a previous school, I set up this, and it works wonders. For administrators: create a Google Classroom for staff teachers, with teachers as teachers, and teachers as students. This is a perfect way for email traffic to be minimized. Conduct fast and effective surveys of workers. Post "assignments" such as plans for professional growth and allow "students" (teachers) to submit when completed. Or post reporting tools and open commentaries so that teachers can view posts as boards of discussion.

SMARTER WAYS TO CLASSROOM GOOGLE

It excels in providing solutions for a wide range of teachers with a variety of expertise and comfort level with the education technology. It also makes use of the familiar Google template that many teachers have used for years. For many teachers right here right now, in many classrooms, it scratches the itch.

CHAPTER 8:

Motivating Students

As a teacher, sometimes you need some good ways to motivate pupils. Here are a few ways that you can help motivate students in an online classroom learning environment.

FRONT ROW MATH PROGRAM

This is a program that was begun by a startup company, and it makes math fun. It involves providing various activities and games for students in grades K-8, and each time this is done, the teachers get progress reports. This is used to help with kids who are struggling early with math and also to help them to not just copy from the books.

Front Row works to change this, creating a tailor-made plan for children so that they can understand math better. It's used today by more than 25,000 different elementary and middle school kids, and you can get either a free or paid version. Using this, teachers get reports on how students are doing, and to help if they have trouble. It helps to give a personalized idea on how to better understand math.

With this app, you're essentially letting students work on both Math, English, Science, and Social Studies lessons since Front Row is a subset of the Freckle Education app. They're given little games based on different concepts, and each student can work at their own pace. Teachers can step in as needed and help students whenever they have trouble. The games are fun, and not just the same blackboard math texts that you may see in a traditional classroom. By making it individualized, you can help those who have fallen behind, and help those who get it to continue forward without making anyone else feel bad.

GOOGLE CLASSROOM BOOK CLUB

This is something that you as a teacher will need to set up, but it's a great way for you to get students to read. A book club helps inspire students to read more. How you can do it, is put together a book club with a code, and from there, set up small challenges. For example, you can have them take pictures of a book that they recently read and say why it's a good read. They can do this with every book they read, and maybe they get a star, and after a certain amount, they get a prize that they like. You can even take this to the next level, such as having students post about it, giving their recommendations, and for extra points, they can have other students respond, and tell you why they liked or didn't like this book. You can keep them going. You can even give incentives by giving them extra points for discussing this in class, telling others about this book. It's a bit of a more hands-on program that you will need to put together, but if you want to motivate a student, sometimes adding in a book club can make a difference.

ENCOURAGE SELF-MONITORING

This is another element of Google Classroom that you can keep in mind. Lots of times, students like to be self-motivated, and you need to make sure that you give them a chance to look at their progress. For example, implementing a backboard can help students improve, and they can look at the discussions, projects, assignments, and the like, and you can have them focus on their progress with Google Classroom as well to make them even more curious about the progress they are making. Putting together discussion forums on Google Classroom, and having students see their grades, are surefire ways to help them get motivated with education in the correct way

ACKNOWLEDGE THE CHALLENGES

When you're trying to get students excited to work on a subject, you should give them a challenge. Once a week, give them a challenge, maybe make it extra credit or something. This can be used to get students interested in working harder. If you acknowledge that it's a challenge, encourage students to find the answer, and offer the right incentive, you should also assure them they can do it.

VIDEO HELP

One thing that you should consider, especially if you're a teacher in a class that doesn't meet a lot, is to make a message for students to see, whether it be a text or even a video message, and place it on the home page. You can get a lot of great results with this, since students will see that the teacher is involved, and that is a big part of some students' ability to work with a class and get the results they want. Being involved is a two-way street, and as a teacher, you should always get students working together.

SCRATCH

Want to get your student's creative juices going while creating a healthy online learning environment? Scratch is a way to do it. This is an MIT site that allows students to make various projects online, and you can export them to others. This is great if you want to help teach students about symmetry and other concepts, and from there, show it to other students. This is a way to get students to be creative, and you can connect it with Google Classroom, have them work with it, and also get them to show it to the teacher for extra credit.

EXTRA CREDIT!

With all of these, the best thing to add is, of course, extra credit. By building these activities, you'll be able to motivate students to do them. Lots of students want to make sure that their grade is intact, and sometimes the best way to ensure that it is, is through extra credit. While some students may prefer to just not do these projects, if their grades are in jeopardy, it may prompt them to start using these activities, and it's a way to encourage them to use the tools as well.

By making sure you motivate students, you'll get them excited to learn, which in turn will help them feel more excited about learning and bettering themselves. If you know how to motivate them, they will do well, and you as a teacher will have a much easier time with your class too.

CHAPTER 9:

Assigning Homework

Assignments are a useful tool on Google Classroom for delivering, tracking, and also grading student submissions. Non-electronic submissions can also be tracked using the Assignments tool.

Add an Assignment

Creating an Assignment:

- Open classroom.google.com.

- At the top, click on Class and open Classwork.

- Also, click on Create and click on Assignment.

- Input the title and necessary instructions.

Posting Assignment:

a. To one or more classes:

- Just below for, click the drawdown on Class.

- Choose the Class you want to include.

b. To individual students:

- Select a class and click the drawdown on All Students

- Uncheck All Students

- Then select the particular student(s)

Inputting grade category:

- Click the drawdown on Grade Category

- Select Category

- Edit the following (Optional):

- Click Grades to edit the grades page

- Click Instructions to compose the Assignment

- Click Classwork to create a homework, quiz, and test

Change the point value:

- Click the drawdown below Points

- Create a new point value or click ungraded

Edit due date or Time:

- Click on the drawdown below Due

- Click on the dropdown on No due date

- Fix date on the Calendar

- Create due Time by clicking Time, input a time adding AM or PM

Add a topic:

- Click on the drawdown below Topic

- Click on Create topic and input the topic name

- Click on an existing Topic to select it

Insert Attachments:
File:

- Click on Attach

- Search for the file and select it

- Click Upload

Drive:

- Click on Drive

- Search for the item and click it

- Click Add

YouTube:

- Click on YouTube

- Type in the keyword on the search bar and click search

- Select the video

- Click Add

For video link by URL:

- Click on YouTube and select the URL

- Input the URL and Add

Link:

- Click on Link

- Select the URL

- Click on Add link

You can delete an attachment:

- Click remove or the cross sign beside it.

You can also determine the number of students that interacts with the Attachment:

- Click on the drawdown besides the Attachment

- Select the required option:

- Students can View File– This implies that students are allowed to read the data but cannot edit it.

- Students can edit the file – This means students can write and share the same data.

- Make a personal copy of each student – This means students can have their transcript with their name on the file and can still have access to it even when turned in until the teacher returns it to them.

Note: If you encounter an issue like, no permission to attach a file, click on copy. This will make the Classroom make a copy, which is attached to the Assignment and saved to the class Drive folder.

ADD A RUBRIC

You must have titled the Assignment before you create a rubric

- Click the Add sign beside Rubric

- Click on Create rubric

- Turn off scoring by clicking the switch to off, besides the Use scoring

- Using scoring is optional, click Ascending or Descending beside the Sort the order of points.

Note: using scoring, gives you the room to add performance level in any, with the levels arranged by point value automatically.

- You can input Criterion like Teamwork, Grammar, or Citations. Click the criterion title

- Add Criterion description (Optional). Click the Criterion description and input the description

Note: You can add multiple performance level and Criterion

- Input points by entering the number of points allotted

Note: The total rubric score auto-updates as points are added

- Add a Level title, input titles to distinguish performance level, e.g., Full Mastery, Excellent, Level A

- Add Descriptions, input expectations for each performance level

- Rearrange Criterion by clicking More and select Up or Down

- Click Save on the right corner to save Rubric

Reuse Rubric:

- Click on the Add sign beside Rubric

- Click Reuse Rubric

- Enter Select Rubric and click on the title. You can select a Rubric from a different class by entering the class name OR by clicking the drawdown and select the Class.

- View or Edit rubric, click on preview, click on Select and Edit to edit, save changes when done. Go back and click Select to view

View rubric assignments:

- Click on Rubric

- Click the arrow up down icon for Expand criteria

- Click the arrow down up icon for Collapse criteria

The grading rubric can be done from the Student work page or the grading tool.

SHARING A RUBRIC

This is possible through export. The teacher creates the Rubric exports, and these are saved to a class Drive called Rubric Exports. This folder can be shared with other teachers and imported into their Assignment.

The imported Rubric can be edited by the teacher in their Assignment, and this editing should not be carried out in the Rubric Exports folder.

Export:

- Click on Rubric
- Click More on the top-right corner and enter Export to Sheets
- Return to Classwork page by clicking close (cross sign) at the top-left corner

- At the top of the Classwork page, click on the Drive folder and enter My Drive
- Select an option, to share one rubric, right-click the Rubric. To share a rubric folder, right-click on the folder.
- After right-clicking, click on Share and input the email you are sharing to.
- Then click Send

Import:

- Click on the Add sign beside Rubric and enter Import from Sheets
- Click on the particular Rubric you want and click on Add
- Edit the Rubric (Optional)
- Click on Save

Editing Rubric Assignment:

- Click on the Rubric
- Click on More at the top-right corner and enter Edit
- Click Save after making changes
- Deleting Rubric Assignment:
- Click on the Rubric
- Click on More at the top-right corner and enter Delete
- Click Delete to confirm

POSTING, SCHEDULING, OR SAVING DRAFT ASSIGNMENT

Post:

- Open Classwork and click on Assignment
- Click on the drawdown beside Assign, on the top-right corner
- Click on Assign to post the Assignment

Schedule:

- Click on the drawdown beside Assign, on the top-right corner
- Enter Schedule
- Input the and date you want the Assignment posted
- Click Schedule

Save:

- Click on the drawdown beside Assign, on the top-right corner
- Enter Save Draft
- Editing Assignment:
- Open Classwork
- Click on More (three-dot) close to Assignment and enter Edit
- Input the changes and save for posted or schedule assignment, while Go to Save draft, to save the draft assignment

Adding Comments to Assignment:

- Open Classwork
- Click Assignment and Enter View Assignment
- Click on Instructions at the top
- Click on Add Class Comment
- Input your comment and Post

To Reuse Announcement and Assignment:

Announcement:

- Open the Class
- Select Stream
- Slide into the Share something with your class box and click on a square clockwise up and down arrow or Reuse post

Assignment:

- Open Classwork and click on Create
- Click on a square clockwise up and down arrow or Reuse post
- Select the Class and Post you want to reuse
- Then click on Reuse

Delete an Assignment:

- Open Classwork
- Click on More (three-dot) close to Assignment
- Click on Delete and confirm the Delete

Creating a Quiz Assignment:

- Open Classwork and click on Create
- Click Quiz Assignment
- Input the title and instructions
- You can switch on Locked mode on Chromebooks to ensure student can't view other pages when taking the quiz
- You can switch on Grade Importing to import grades
- Response and Return of Grades:

Response:

- Open Classwork
- Click on Quiz Assignment and free Quiz Attachment
- Click on Edit and input Response

Return:

- Open Classwork
- Click on Quiz Assignment
- Pick the student and click on Return
- Confirm Return

PLANNING LESSONS

If you are a teacher that manages different classes, this will make classroom management so much easier, which in turn will help with learning, and you do not need to worry so much about juggling the lesson plans for each class.

You can re-use the existing assignments and questions that you tried in another class, and you can also share posts and announcements with so many different classes, which makes it so much easier, and if you have references that you want to use, you can always archive them, so that next year you can go in, get the same posts, and then use them with the same class as well.

But there's even more, if you have a co-teacher, you can have them sign in and help you out with this, and you can invite another teacher that can help you with the learning aspects of the classroom.

This is super great since you do not have to spend as much time trying to put together lesson plans, and if you have multiple teachers helping, it can make everything a lot easier.

Finally, you can create class resources pages.

This is awesome for those teachers that have to deal with many of the different issues that come from trying to get all of their students the information that they need.

This resources page has everything all in the right place, so if they need extra info, especially video and other learning resources information, then this is the perfect thing for them, and it can make it much easier for teachers too.

With Google Classroom, everything is made easier, and you can get the full benefits of what you can use, and in turn, help out more students than ever before.

SCHEDULING

Scheduling and reusing posts are something teachers do, especially if they have an assignment that they liked. To schedule a post, you can create it so that it appears at a time and date. To do this, you press the option to create a post or assignment, and then on the side, you'll see a tab that has a plus sign on it. Press that, and you'll then be given the option to schedule this. From there, you can put in when it should appear on the stream, and then it'll happen. You can then finish up, and there you go. This is great for teachers that don't want to have to spend copious amounts of time schedules.

HOW TO KEEP THE STUDENT FOCUSED

The due dates for assignments usually provide extra motivation and focus for students when compared to assignments without due dates. Due dates motivate students to get the work done and not keep on procrastinating. Set reasonable due dates for assignments given. This will motivate students to get the work done.

Setting due dates is easy:

- Create the Assignment

- Type in the title, instructions, and upload any attachments if need be

- On the right-hand side of the panel, there is a tab for Due Date

- Click on the tab and select a due date for the assignment

- Click on Create

- Use Private Comments to Give and Receive Feedback

Google Classroom has the private comment feature which allows you to make comments on student work and give feedback on their performance. This is important because it provides a clear path for confidential two-way communication. You can use this feature to directly motivate students by giving helpful comments and encouraging them to perform better. Nothing motivates a student more than encouragement and praise from a teacher. Praise students in private comments when necessary to motivate them to do better. Private comments can be referred to at any time hence help students to remember your helpful comments.

Here's how private comments are added from the Student Work page:

- Start at the Classwork tab; select the assignment on which you will love to make a private comment.

- Click View Assignment

- Select the student whose work you wish to comment on from the roster on the left of the screen.

- Click on the Add Private Comment button. It is at the bottom of the right-hand panel.

- Click on it to type your comment.

- You can also make private comments while grading students' assignments. Follow these steps to add private comments as you grade assignments.

- Start at the Classwork tab. Click on the assignment you want to give a private comment on.

- Click View Assignment.

- Select the student's file you would want to comment on.

- Use the panel on the right side of the screen to post a comment.

- Add Quizzes to Make things More Fun

You can create quizzes on your Google Classroom environment. Quizzes provide a source for added engagement. They can motivate the students to learn in a fun way as well. Creating Quizzes is easy to do within the Google Classroom environment.

CHAPTER 10:

Google Classroom Extensions And Apps Available

CLASSDOJO

CLASSDOJO allows teachers to vary actions in their classes quickly and simply. The extensions and apps to the Google Extensions and apps every Teacher should learn. It tracks and produces habit data which will be shared by teachers with parents and managers."

GOOGLE KEEP

"Catch what you think and share these thoughts with your family and friends. Talk a voice memo on the go and obtain it transcribed automatically."

GLOGSTER EDU

'GLOGSTER EDU' allows you to build Glugs – online multimedia posters – with text, pictures, graphics, sounds, links, sketches, data attachments'

SKETCHPAD

"You can play with images by incorporating new elements into the composition, inserting notes, changing graphics, overlaying text on something, or going back and forwards in time forever through the changes you create ."

VOICENOTE II: SPEECH TO TEXT

Typing together with your voice and speech recognition, it's a functional and easy notepad."

ANYDO

"ANYDO is employed by over 10 million people to coordinate everything they need to try to.

PIX1R EXPRESS

PIX1R Express" may be a powerful and fun photo editor that permits you to quickly create, resize, and alter any image with a completely ad-free experience. Choose between quite 2 million free effects, overlays, and borders combinations to personalize your pictures further. You appear as if a professional, albeit you've never edited a photograph before once you are PIX1R Express."

PIX1R -0- MATIC

"PIX1R -o-MATIC is an amusing and easy-to-use photography/darkroom tool to feature effects, overlays, and borderlines to your images easily.

If you would like to seem vintage, grunge, clean, or trendy, PIX1R -o- MATIC makes it easy in three simple ways, and you'll never begin of the latest styles with quite 2 million editing combinations to settle on that make your pictures look stunning."

DICTANOTE

"DICTANOTE offers you a highly advanced text editor and integrated multilingual speaker recognition." Auto Text Expander

Auto Text Expander allows you to shortcut into emails for lengthy texts. In reaction to the parent or student inquiries about their grade, for instance, maybe you furthermore may type

"Thank You for your email." you'll create a shortcut with Auto Text Expander, like 'TY,' which automatically inserts the text you wish. You'll find out various alternatives supported text bits, which you regularly use. It allows you to write emails and answer emails you receive efficiently.

CHECKMARK

Checkmark is an extension that allows you to leave quick feedback on Google Docs for a student's article. Rather than typing out all of the comments you would like to feature, you'll make any comments that you only often make in student papers like "new paragraph," "run-on," or "comma mistake" and insert your comment easily.

Then a little box with the choices for feedback will appear, pick the correct explanation, and it'll be added automatically. You are doing to have the proper to form additional notes, but Checkmark can assist you with correct feedback in grading papers more quickly.

GOOBRIC + DOCTOPUS

GOOBRIC and DOCTOPUS work together and work exceptionally well with Google Classroom. DOCTOPUS pulls ties to every task in Google Classroom assignments and essays. GOOBRIC helps you to make a rubric during which each document is often opened. You'll build your products or use the models in GOOBRIC. GOOBRIC opens a page once you open a student assignment and GOOBRIC simultaneously, so you'll click on the boxes of the element you would like to hitch, so leave the comments. GOOBRIC adds and offers a mean ranking, so it can notify the scholar that their assignment is marked and prepared for Display.

POCKET

Pocket is an extension to save lots of products, videos, and websites you'd wish to visit. After downloading Pocket, you only press the extension in your Chrome browser once you come to a video or site that you simply want to recollect, and Pocket saves it to you. You'll access all the blogs, videos, and articles you've got saved when logging into Pocket. It's an ideal thanks to keeping track of stuff you would like for future lessons or professional growth.

SCREENCASTIFY

SCREENCASTIFY is an extension that allows you to video something on your screen. It's unique because you'll open your laptop with an internet site or article rather than having to form PDF versions of all that you simply want in your photo.

You'll even prefer to record the Open tab, the whole monitor, or maybe add your webcam to your video within the lower corner after downloading and opening SCREENCASTIFY. You'll also use your mouse to write down and highlight multiple parts of your screen once you begin recording. You'll save your video to your Google Drive, where students and staff can share it. It's especially useful for eLearning or updating your LMS lessons.

Hopefully, these Google Chrome teachers' extensions can assist you rate and interact more effectively.

HIDDEN FEATURES

THE ASSIGNMENT CALENDAR

Google Classroom consequently makes an Assignment Calendar to assist and keep understudies and educators composed. Whenever a teacher creates a task or question within Google Classroom and connects a maturity to that, the work directly shows on the category schedule within Google Classroom.

To discover this schedule, select the three lines within the upper left corner of the screen and eventually choose the calendar. With this screen shown, educators and understudies can see work that has been apportioned to the category.

Educators will likewise see that another Calendar currently shows up in their G Suite Calendar. Not exclusively, would teachers be ready to add assignments to the present schedule through the classroom?

Yet, they will likewise straightforwardly get to it through G Suite Calendar to incorporate occasions for the category which will not be attached to maturity. A couple of instances of instructors utilizing this schedule work include booking class field trips, fixing additional mentoring time, and composing an after-school meeting. To form the schedule progressively available, consider making it open within the Calendar settings and eventually sharing the URL interface with guardians.

THE WORK AREA

Educators and understudies can likewise exploit the Work region within Google Classroom to accumulate every exceptional task into one area. On the off chance that a teacher has not evaluated a selected job, it'll show immediately. Thus, if an understudy has not turned during a task, it'll likewise show in their Work region. During this way, the Work territory can fill in as a defector task list and may support educators and understudies to differentiate and affect their work process adequately.

ORGANIZE THE CATEGORY STREAM WITH TOPICS

Subjects another component within Google Classroom and permits educators to mapped out the presentations that they add on the Classroom "Stream." When making a declaration, task, or question, instructors would now be ready to administer some extent. These points set about as a classification for every post, which allows them to be composed proficiently.

At the purpose when another subject is formed, it'll show on the left half the Classroom Stream and, when a topic is chosen, all posts that are apportioned that time will show up. The Topics highlight currently permits instructors to mapped out everything of the substance within their course. As an example, a history instructor may make some extent for each unit of study, for instance, "Old Rome." A math educator may plan to make a topic for each group or part that they study.

SHARE TO CLASSROOM EXTENSION

For educators utilizing Chromebooks or workstations in their classrooms, the Share to Classroom Chrome Extension permits instructors to point out and offer understudy work and screens effectively with the category. Using the Share to Classroom expansion, understudies can share an internet site with their educator's PC. Within the first place, understudies click the extension, then they select Push to Teacher. When done, the educator gets a warning on her screen that she should acknowledge before the understudy's page will show.

By following similar advances, a teacher can obtrude an internet site to their understudies' gadgets continuously!

The expansion likewise permits educators to form Google Classroom content right from the augmentation. If a teacher finds an internet site he might want to post in Google Classroom as a feature of a task, question, or declaration, he can make any of these alternatives by using the augmentation.

By utilizing the Share to Classroom expansion, instructors and understudies are presently able to share new disclosures and stories effectively and successfully.

Wrapping it up, while Google Classroom is notable for arranging understudy add Google Drive, making singular duplicates of Google Docs, and checking out digital substance. These three underused highlights of Google Classroom can support you and your understudies become significantly progressively effective when utilizing innovation within the Classroom!

CHAPTER 11:

Google Hangouts For Video Conferencing

G oogle Hangouts Chat is a free online chat system for individual and group chats.

MAKE DISTANCE LEARNING OPEN TO ALL STUDENTS

One of the most troublesome difficulties of instructing is fitting the necessities of each student. That challenge is made progressively complicated when you (and your co-educators) can't work with students face to face.

Google Classroom permits you to make one of a kind assignments for people or little gatherings of students. You can make special learning exercises dependent on the alterations required by IEPs or 504 plans – just as modifications for students who are English Language Learners.

These students are probably going to confront noteworthy difficulties in progressing out of the typical everyday practice of face to face school, so your remote class must address the issues.

For instructors planning for potential school terminations—or presently confronting them—here are a couple of different approaches to deal with distance learning.

KEEP ON ASSOCIATING WITH HANGOUTS MEET

At the point when students' schedules are disturbed, many acknowledge that they miss the structure of school and learning with their instructor. It can help maintain that sentiment of solace and security during a period of vulnerability.

Scheduling is another problem that can arise. Using the Calendar Appointment Slots, students who need extra support will sign up to meet one on one or in small groups with you. Owing to intermittent or lack of Wi-Fi connectivity, or changing childcare options, not all students can enter a virtual classroom at the same time. Your teaching would likely be a combination of live video and posting videos of your lessons for students who couldn't make it. Fortunately, unique features in Hangouts Meet enable you to record your lessons to share with students.

CHECK-IN WITH HOW YOUR STUDENTS ARE FEELING

Social-Emotional Learning can proceed effectively. As you can utilize Hangouts Meet to "be" there for your students and keep up your homeroom culture, you can give different approaches to students to help their feelings while away from school.

It's not normal.

Google does, however, offer Hangouts Meet premium features free of charge to teachers and students who are at home during the coronavirus pandemic, allowing virtual meetings of up to 250 people as well as live streaming.

Besides, to live video capabilities, the Hangouts Meet recording feature provides teachers with a simple way to make pre-recorded lesson videos for students to watch on their own time.

PARENT-TEACHER COMMUNICATION IS SO EASY

Talking about classes, Hangouts is ideal for busy guardians. They can send a speedy message to you to plan a video gathering, and you can meet with them (on the web, obviously!) whenever it's helpful for both of you.

On the other hand, you can keep a Google Calendar for parents to plan their meetings so that there are huge amounts of potential outcomes.

Keeping guardians educated is a significant part of student achievement and these are some extremely simple approaches to do that.

CONNECT WITH HANGOUTS MEET

When students' routines are interrupted, many recognize how much they miss the structure of school and interacting with their teacher. It's essential to preserve that sense of comfort and safety throughout uncertainty.

CHAPTER 12:

Love Your Job As An Online Tutor

Being a teacher is an extremely rewarding career. However, there are times it can be stressful and disappointed even under normal circumstances, and dealing with COVID-19 has compounded that effect. If you find your love for teaching being hurt by recent events, take this time to reflect and rekindle your love for the occupation. This chapter is dedicated to helping you love your job as much as you did when you decided to pursue this career even during this trying time. Doing this will allow you to give maximum benefit to your students as you impact knowledge, wisdom, and education through this new online medium.

BECOME MORE MINDFUL

Many things can cause a teacher to become burnt out, from working under stressful conditions and working with difficult students with physiological and learning problems. COVID-19 has compounded the stresses associated with this job, and this can leave a teacher feel adrift and unsure about how they feel about their jobs. Embracing mindful practice will allow the teacher to become more aware of the emotions that they feel so that they can learn to manage these emotions in a positive and conducive way. COVID-19 does not have to take away your passion for teaching and being more mindful can help ensure that your power as an educator stays with you even during this global crisis.

Mindfulness is the practice of focusing your awareness on the present moment so that you can wholly embrace and accept your thoughts, feelings, and bodily sensations. Being mindful is a threefold process that involves:

- Paying attention to what is happening right now in the present moment.
- Paying attention to the present moment deliberately and purposely with absolute resolve.
- Having the resolve to maintain an attitude that allows you to stay present at the moment whether or not the moment is pleasant or unpleasant.

COVID-19 has us looking back horrified on the past and worrying about the future. Ground yourself in the present and find happiness within yourself and as an educator by being more mindful.

Mindfulness is not a practice that you can just pull out of a hat every time you need it. It is something that you need to continually practice for it to be effective. Practice mindfulness every day and you will find yourself more settled in your awareness of yourself, your emotions, and thoughts. Being mindful is not something that will take up a lot of time as you practice making it an ingrained part of yourself. It only takes a few minutes and as it becomes a habit, you will not even notice that you are doing it.

A few ways in which you can practice mindfulness every day include:

- Simply taking a few minutes during the day to put aside everything else and taking a few slow breaths to notice how air moves in and out of your body.
- Practicing S.T.O.P. - *S*top, *take* a breath, *observe* what you are feeling then *P*roceed—when you feel overwhelmed.
- Practicing mindful meditation.
- Paying attention to the bodily sensations you experience when you do simple tasks like brushing your teeth.

Education specific actions that you can take to become more mindful every day include noticing how you feel when you perform education-specific tasks, such as typing in Google Docs as you develop your online curriculum and practicing mindful breathing when you feel overwhelmed by the situation of learning to teach your class online.

PRACTICE GRATITUDE

Embracing a grateful attitude will go a long way in helping you cope with this COVID-19 pandemic as well as allow you to get in touch with your love for teaching. If there is one thing that this pandemic show is that there is so much to be grateful for in life, and you can find meaning and value in even the smallest things.

The benefits of practicing gratitude include:
- Boosting your immune system.
- Allowing you to better cope with stress.
- Lowering your risk of developing mental health issues, such as depression and anxiety.

Practicing gratitude as a professional educator is rewarding, fun and it does not require that you do elaborate tasks or actions. All you need is a notebook, a pen, and you are all set to practice gratitude and gain the benefits listed above and more. This is known as gratitude journaling.

All you have to do to practice it is:

- Find a calming, relaxing, and quiet environment to sit.
- Ponder on all the good things that are going on in your life, especially when it comes to your educational career. Write three of them down in your journal.
- Write three things that you enjoy about teaching in your journal.
- Write three things that you are looking forward to in the future as it pertains to your educational career.
- Name two people who have helped you or encourage pursue teaching and to continue with the career.
- Name the two of the accomplishments that you have made so far in allowing you to adjust to this new environment of education.

Do this exercise several times a week, and you will find that you can pinpoint the things that you are grateful for as an educator more clearly and therefore find more happiness and joy in the career, especially during this trying global crisis.

Another great way of practicing gratitude as an educator is to count your blessings before you go to sleep instead of counting sheep. Keeping the great things that you love about being an educator in your mind just before you go to sleep makes it more likely that you get up pumped and ready to teach your students the next morning.

MAKE SELF-CARE A PRIORITY

The needs when it comes to the physical, mental, emotional, and spiritual health of educators often get pushed under the rug, even when we function under normal circumstances. This can seem triply, so when everyone is trying to adapt to a new schedule and a different way of imparting education to students. You can truly feel the pressure as an educator as you tried to balance the needs of your family, friends, personal life, and more along with your dedication to teaching and your students.

This overwhelm can lead to self-neglect, but the only way that you can give your best to teaching is to ensure that you are caring for your well-being and ensure that your overall health is a top priority. Self-care needs to be a priority even more now that there are so many physical and psychological pressures being introduced by this COVID-19 pandemic.

One of the best ways to practice self-care is to set personal and maintain personal boundaries for yourself. We now live in a society where many people work from home and that includes educators that facilitate online education for students. Where there were set working hours for most teachers before the COVID-19 pandemic, this is no longer so since we have introduced conditions that allow persons to work from home. Therefore, schedules can become blurred with no clear start time and end time. This can quickly lead to burnout if healthy working hours are not maintained. Schedule your working hours in your Google Calendar, and also ensure that you put time for breaks.

Learning what is within your control and what is outside of your control is essential for self-care as well. COVID-19 has placed many people in a constant state of worry and anxiety about things they can do nothing about. Both of these conditions can lead to dire physical, mental, and emotional health consequences. Allow yourself to gain perspective by recognizing that some things are just not within your control. Recognize that it is healthier to focus on the things that are within your control, such as meeting the demands of educating your students through distance learning.

It is also important that you establish a self-care routine that includes a daily, weekly, and monthly schedule. Such a schedule should include time for self-reflection, eating healthily, exercising, gratitude journaling, and more. You also have control of nurturing your love for education.

KEEP IN TOUCH AND COLLABORATE WITH OTHER EDUCATORS

Collaborating and communicating with other educators has a way of reminding you that there is much to love about the profession. Therefore, it is pertinent to keep in touch with other educators, even those who teach outside of the subject areas that you educate in. Whereas you would have had open communication and human interaction with teachers in a staff room in a physical environment, you now have to find other ways of keeping the connection with your colleagues and other educators.

Despite the need for social distancing, there are still ways that you can do this and maintain that human interaction. Such ways include:

- Developing an online social network. There are several ways in which people can connect online, including chatting in forums, on social media websites like educator-related Facebook pages and groups, and more. Simple things like seeing a funny meme dedicated to the practice teaching on your social media feed can brighten your day and help you feel more connected with your peers.

- Collaborate with your colleagues to develop lesson plans and curriculum for the upcoming school year.

- Schedule weekly meetups with colleagues. In many areas, governments have not stipulated that a total lockdown is in effect, only that persons practice proper social distancing techniques. Therefore, you can meet up with colleagues as long as you implement these recommended protocols. This is a great time to seek advice from other teachers and work on projects together.

- Embrace co-teaching. It is possible to share the responsibilities of maintaining a class with another teacher, even in an online environment. Doing so will mean a regular interaction with another teacher and, therefore, integrate that human touch for teachers with distance learning.

USE YOUR GOOGLE CLASSROOM TO MOTIVATE BOTH YOURSELF AND YOUR STUDENTS

Despite the many challenges that can come with being an educator, many teachers love their jobs simply because of the huge impact that they have on other people and the fact that they help students set up their future. Therefore, it only makes sense that you use this motivation to help you rekindle or keep the spark alive that you have for teaching. Motivate your students to do their best at online learning so you can feel empowered by their progress.

Ways in which you can do this include:

- Use goal setting with students so that they complete a certain amount of assigned classwork every week. You can motivate them to do this by weekly certificates or a points system that allows them to see their progress.
- Use positive reinforcement with rewards and praise. You can do this by using announcements and the private comments features in Google Classroom. Make this fun by using emojis, motivational quotes, GIFs, videos, and

more. You can also send regular emails that simply motivate students.

- Take the time to chat off-topic with your students so that they can have a much-needed break from schooling every once in a while. This can be done via video conferencing, such as with Google Meet.

WORK SMARTER TO MAKE ONLINE LEARNING SUCCESS RATHER THAN HARDER

Constantly going at it full hundred will leave you burnt out and not loving your career as a teacher. Therefore, working harder is not the answer. Working smart is. You need to develop ways and systems to make your workload lighter in this phase of online learning so that you can take time to ensure the fruits of your labor as an educator. The first thing you need to do is let go of the idea of perfection. Perfection is a myth and never achievable, especially in a chaotic time, like during a worldwide pandemic. There will be hiccups and mishaps along the way as you learn to adjust to this new way of education. Accept them and make peace with it. Also, learn to prioritize. You cannot do everything at once. Do the most important things first.

Other ways you can work smarter with Google Classroom include:

- Setting up systems and routines for your online classes.
- Add other teachers to your Google Classroom to lessen your workload.

- Digitize your assignments by scanning and uploading them to Google Classroom instead of trying to recreate them online.

CONTINUOUSLY PURSUE CONTINUED KNOWLEDGE IN ONLINE EDUCATION

The brain loves stimulation and there is no better way to ignite the fire of your love for teaching by continually feeding your brain information about your occupation. You can do this in a variety of ways, such as taking formal courses and classes, reading books, watching videos, and even simpler tasks like browsing the Internet.

CHAPTER 13:

Creative Ways To
Use Google Classroom To Teach

TEACHING MATH

I f you are thinking about how else you can expand the experience of learning math or using Classroom in your math classes, here are some creative ways to build on.

THE PROBLEM OF THE WEEK

Aptly known as POW, POWs can be anything that you feel needs more attention. It can be a problem you have identified or a problem that your students can identify. You can create games that can help students learn about the problem differently and participating students can submit their work directly to Google Classroom.

NUMBER LINES

1. **Make each line add up to 16.**

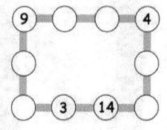

2. **Make each line add up to 20.**

LINK INTERACTIVE SIMULATIONS

There are several websites dedicated to providing helpful math simulations. Sites like *Explore Learning* have thousands of math simulations and math variations that students can look up to solve mathematical problems. You can link these URLs in your classroom either as part of an assignment or through an Announcement.

LINK TO PLAYSHEETS

Playsheets fall between gamification and GBL. Teachers can link up relevant *Playsheets* and give these assignments to the students. These playsheets give immediate feedback to students, and it is an excellent learning and motivational tool that tells the students that they are on the right track.

USE GOOGLE DRAW

Google Draw is another creative tool that allows students and teachers to create virtual manipulations such as charts, Algebra tiles, and so on. Draw images that make it easy for students to identify with Math. This can be used to create differentiated assignments targeting students with different learning levels.

USE DIGITAL TOOLS

Digital tools such as *Desmos*, *Geogebra*, and *Daum Equation Editor* can also be used to solve various math problems. These tools can be used from Google Drive and integrated with other Google documents. Once done, students can submit their solved problems to Google Classroom.

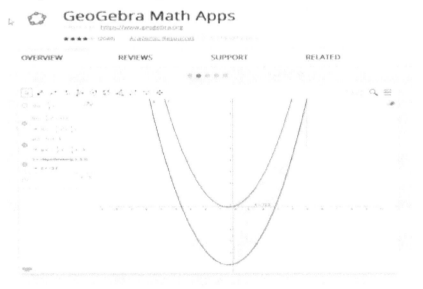

TEACH PROGRAMMING

Get students to use programs such as *Scratch* or *Google Apps Script* that can enable them to exhibit their understanding of mathematical concepts.

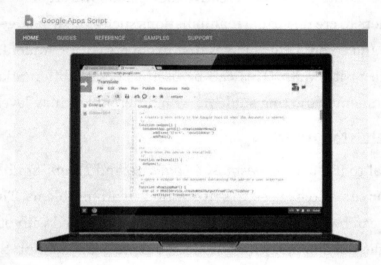

TEACHING SCIENCE

HANGOUT WITH EXPERTS

Get experts you are connected to in real life to talk about their experiences working in a science-related field to help students with their science-related subjects. You can use Google Hangouts to send questions the class has and link it to your Google Classroom. This enables the students to access the Hangout and participate in the questioning or even watch the interview after the session is done. The Hangout Session can be archived for later viewing.

COLLECTING EVIDENCE

Have your students submit 'evidence' of science experiments by sending in photos or videos of their science projects and uploading it to Google Classroom.

GIVE REAL-LIFE EXAMPLES

Tailor-made your science projects and assignments so that it gets students to go outside and get real-life samples that they can record on their mobile devices. They can take these images and submit it immediately to the Google Classroom. Make it interesting, students that submit their answers faster get extra points!

CROWDSOURCING INFORMATION

Get students into the whole idea and activity of crowdsourcing. Create a Google Spreadsheet with a specific topic and specify what information they need and what goals the project needs to accomplish. Upload the document to Google Classroom and get students to find and contribute information.

TEACHING WRITING & READING

PROVIDE TEMPLATES

Allow students to access writing templates on Google Classroom for things such as formal letters, informal letters, report writing, assignment templates, resumes, and cover letter formats.

READING RECORDS

Establish a *weekly reading record* on Google Classroom where they can record information on the times that they have read during the week. So instead of writing it down on a reading diary, allow them to update a form on Google Classroom by entering the necessary data. This allows them to immediately add in the information of the books that they have read while it is still fresh in their minds.

Class Reading Record

Tom Barrett
ICT in my Classroom - http://tbarrett.edublogs.org

Name

Date

Book Title

Page Numbers

Comments
What did you enjoy? Did you struggle with any words? What help did you get?

I read with...

Submit

COLLABORATE ON WRITING PROJECTS

Get your students to collaborate on writing projects via Group assignments.

These projects can be anything from preparing newspaper articles, journals, e-portfolios, and so on.

Spelling Tests

You can create a simple 1-10 or 1-20 *weekly spelling test* via Google Form. Get students to type in their answers as you read out the list of words. Once completed, apply a formula to judge if they are correct or not, and it becomes self-marking.

Spelling Test

Tom Barrett
ICT in my Classroom http://tbarrett.edublogs.org

Name

1)

2)

3)

4)

5)

6)

8)

Teaching Physical Education

Didn't think PE could be done via Google Classroom? Here are some ideas:

Post Fitness Videos

Post fitness videos to help your students understand how to perform a workout. Send out videos to any psychical activity that you want students to conduct on their next PE session, or you can also just post a video after classes so students can practice the exercise in their own time and work on their form.

Get students to post videos of their daily workout

Have your students post videos in the public feed on your Google Classroom with a hashtag such as #midweekfitspo. Encourage students to work out and post their videos each week.

Link to safety videos

Post up safety videos for your PE activities, so your students know what kind of skills they need to follow to exercise safely.

Post Resources for activities

PE teachers can also post useful resources for games and activities ahead of time such as rules and methods of playing before the student's next PE session.

It would help the students prepare and know what to expect for their next class.

CREATE A FITNESS TRACKER

Assign students to a *Fitness Tracker spreadsheet* and make a copy for each student. Assign a due date for the end of the semester for their physical education class. You can monitor each student's progress by checking out the assignment folder in the Google Classroom.

Use the spreadsheet to get your students to track their progress. Whenever students update their results, the spreadsheet automatically updates to dynamic charts so students can see their progress visually over the entire semester.

You can either pair students up to work in partners or individually. Get the students to take photos of each other's forms when practicing certain tasks so that you can evaluate their form and correct it by way of giving them feedback via Classroom or during PE classes. A rubric would be helpful here too so that students can self-evaluate their workouts and make corrections where necessary.

OTHER TEACHING METHODS TO USE

ATTACH PATTERNS AND STRUCTURES

Upload patterns and structures that students can identify and explain. Students can also collaborate with other students to identify patterns and structures to come up with solutions.

USE GEOMETRIC CONCEPTS

Use Google Drawings or Slides to insert drawings of geometric figures for math, science, and even for art.

COLLABORATE ONLINE WITH OTHER TEACHERS

If you know other teachers have modules or projects which would come in handy with your class, collaborate, and enable your students to join in as well. Different teachers allow for different resources, and the teaching load can also be distributed.

PEER TUTORING

Senior students can also be allowed to access your Google Classroom at an agreed time weekly to tutor and give support to junior students or students in differentiated assignments.

CELEBRATE SUCCESS

Google Classroom also enables the teacher to encourage students through comments whenever they submit an assignment because feedback can be given immediately, and this can be done either privately or publicly.

DIGITAL QUIZZES

Quizzes can be used for various subjects on Google Classroom. Get your students to submit their answers quickly for extra points.

SHARE PRESENTATIONS

Share presentations and slides with your students to help them with whatever assignments you have given them.

CHAPTER 14:

Google Classroom Vs Other Platforms

APPLE CLASSROOM VS. GOOGLE CLASSROOM

Apple Classroom is an educational product from Apple. Many educators believe they are the same thing from different companies.

While they have similar names and are built to bring technology to the classroom, there are several differences between both products. Here is how both products compare.

APPLE CLASSROOM

Apple Classroom was launched in March 2016 bringing Apple closer to education. Apple Classroom is available as a free app for Apple iPads and iPhones as well as online. Apple allows the teacher to monitor students' work from an iPad or Mac computer allowing for classroom management. Students' privacy is secure as class records are kept private. Students are notified when the teacher views or projects their screen. With Apple Classroom, a student must not own the devices they use. It works perfectly with iPads with multiple users (shared devices).

Using Apple Classroom, teachers can connect to nearby devices and assign students to shared iPads and log them out of the device after a class. Teachers can monitor and control students' work by starting or pausing student work. The teacher has strong control over student devices and can launch web pages, apps, or documents on student devices from his device. The teacher can also lock the device on a single app, view student activity on the app, or mute audio on student devices.

One downside of Apple Classroom is that this product is limited to only Apple devices. Students will have Apple devices for it to work. Apple Classroom however easily syncs with Google apps and solutions. With Apple Classroom you can easily project items from your iPad into larger Apple TV screens and use Airplay. You can integrate games from third party sources in Apple Classroom.

Teachers can reset forgotten passwords. The teacher also can split the class into groups to carry out projects and tasks. This can be done directly from the teacher's app before being pushed to the students.

Google Classroom

GOOGLE CLASSROOM

Google Classroom works across almost all devices. Teachers and students can use android and non-android devices to access Google Classroom. There is no limitation to what sort of device they can use. This ability to integrate across devices, platforms, and even apps and other similar programs make Google Classroom stands out. You have hundreds of apps and extensions you can add to make your Google Classroom experience more powerful.

Google Classroom stands out for its superb workflow management. Its integration with Google productivity apps and other third-party apps allows the teacher to connect with students in a way few other solutions can. This teacher-student connection allows work to flow from the teacher's Google Drive to the student's Google Drive and vice versa.

Google Classroom makes sharing information easier when compared to other Learning Systems like Apple Classroom. On Google Classroom, digital resources can be easily shared with students. Important resources can be shared on the stream which serves a tool to streamline, house, and archive important information.

The integration with other productivity tools from Google helps users integrate due dates from assignments into Google calendars. This allows the Calendar to be viewed across devices and when customized by other parties like parents. The ease of bringing materials from outside Google Classroom puts it miles ahead of similar software.

From the above comparisons, you will be able to tell the major differences between Apple Classroom and Google Classroom.

Apple Classroom provides stronger classroom management rights to the teacher. The teacher has greater control over student devices with Apple Classroom. It is however limited by the fact that it can only work when the teacher and students own Apple Devices, unlike Google Classroom that is not device-dependent.

Google Classroom's ability to seamlessly integrate with Google productivity tools and third-party apps gives it a winning edge. While Google Classroom and Apple Classroom are both used in the classrooms, they have different objectives. The teacher can, however, make use of both to achieve better learning in the classroom.

NEW FEATURES OF GOOGLE CLASSROOM

As Google Classroom has enjoyed more widespread use, new features and benefits have come out. These are meant to make it easier for both teachers and students to get more out of this platform and for them to find it easier to use. Some of the most recent updates to the Classroom include:

- Quizlet Class—with this update, the teacher can create a Quizlet at the same time they create the class. Once the account is set up, you can set up the Quizlet account and link both of these together. When students join the class, Quizlet will notify them at the same time.
- Upload playing tests—this one is useful for music classes. Students will be able to record playing tests or upload one they have already done. The teacher can then view the playing test and leave their feedback. Students can choose to listen to the test again to make improvements or ask questions if something doesn't make sense to them.

- Outside of class viewing parties—many live events can help with a particular topic, but which may be hard to take the whole class too. For example, live performances, debates, speeches, and even movies could help the teacher talk about certain points. If these live events happen after class hours, the teacher can incorporate them into the class and add live posts and discussions to keep students working together.

- Warm-up questions—if the teacher would like to assess how well students understood the class or perhaps do a quick review before a test, the warmup question feature can help. Post the questions and let students either put in an essay answer or multiple choice. This feature doesn't allow students to see other answers, so you know how each one thinks without influence from their peers.

- Flubaroo—this is a great add-on that allows some homework assignments and tests to be graded immediately. Assignments that use multiple choice questions and true and false statements will enjoy Flubaroo because students can submit the work and receive feedback right away. This saves time for the teacher, allows students to see which questions they got wrong, and speeds up the learning process.

- Class discussions—one cool feature of the Classroom is the ability to have several classes talk together. Teachers can connect with other teachers in the same, or similar classes and students can share ideas and discussions.

- Photo assignments—Classroom can even be used on a smartphone and tablet so students can use their cameras to complete projects. Send students on a scavenger hunt, let them upload a picture of their homework, or use the camera in another way.

- Forums—Forums are another way to expand on the class discussion, making it easy for a whole grade level to converse together and share their knowledge. The school can set up several teachers and administrators to watch the comments of the whole school. Younger students can ask questions about which classes to take, for example, and older students can find out about colleges, how their credits work, and so on.

- Poll questions—all teachers can use a poll question, but it works particularly well for math teachers. They can turn a math problem into a poll so that students can use the skills they learn in class to come up with an answer. This feature also works well for teachers to gather feedback.

- Guided reading—test vocabulary, have students answer questions as they get through parts of a reading assignment, and help make sure important concepts are understood by the whole class before moving on.

- Post a link—posting links can bring in outside sources for students to learn even more. The teacher can add digital resources and videos.

- Parent support—Google has added a feature that allows teachers to communicate with and keep parents up to date on student progress. The parents will need to sign up for the class and then will receive a weekly update and email digests so that they can keep track of upcoming assignments, all important announcements, and how well their student is doing in class. This makes it easier for parents to participate in learning without taking up valuable teacher time.

- Teacher control—teachers, have full control over the classroom. They will be able to decide when something is appropriate and may need to ooGstep in if comments don't stay on topic or students begin to attack each other. The classroom has made this easy for the teacher to control what is going on at all times.

As time goes on, Google Classroom will add on more great features that make it easier for teachers and students to work together inside and outside the classroom. Teachers can already enjoy the ability to be in charge of the Classroom, posting important announcements, handing out assignments without wasting time and paper, and communicating with students. Students will enjoy how easy it is to keep track of their assignments and announcements, the instant feedback on tests and some assignments, and the ability to ask questions when they need clarification. In a world where education is always changing and time is valuable, Google Classroom could be the answer that schools need to get the work done without all the stress and wasted time.

CHAPTER 15:

7 Tips And Tricks For Managing Your Class

Let's look at the best tips for you to organize your classroom.

ORGANIZE ASSIGNMENTS WITH "TOPICS"

This is a simple means of organizing data in Google Classroom. It is the foundation on which all other organizations are founded on the platform. Topics help you to bring tasks and tools into categories that learners can reach easily and efficiently. Here are six ways to organize assignments.

ORGANIZE BY UNIT

Teachers establish topics for each unit to classify by unit of study and put all assignments for that specific unit inside that topic.

ORGANIZE WEEKLY

With each week, teachers can build a new topic, either calling them "Week # 1," or calling anything like, "September 10-14 week."

ORGANIZE BY TYPE

Instructors arrange tasks in this system by task category, such as "Daily Activity," "Projects," "Tests," etc. Know the company is for you and your pupils alike. Remember to make things for the age category you instruct.

ORGANIZE BY AREA

For elementary school teachers, who teach several topics, grouping by topic area appears to be the most appropriate.

ORGANIZE BY DAY

Normally, this approach is paired with one of the strategies above. The aim is to build a specific topic entitled "Today," where anything you want learners to focus on the day is transferred manually. Then push the "Today" issue to the top of the page for students to see clearly.

ORGANIZE BY GOAL

Even if you don't have standard-based scoring, this is a perfect opportunity to help the students align the task with the assignment goal.

Conclusion

G oogle Classroom may have a lot of competition in the market, but this does not mean it cannot hold up against the rest. Classroom combines a lot of your favorite Google apps into one to help make it easier than ever, to create lesson plans, send out assignments, provide feedback to students in real-time and sometimes immediately, and to alert your students of any notifications and announcements that are important to the class.

Google Classroom and other learning applications will never replace our teachers, but these tools can help them improve every aspect of learning.

Students can use the Classroom to easily complete assignments, ask any questions that they have, read announcements, and participate in any of the discussions or group work that is required. With a valid Gmail address and an invitation from the teacher, it is easier than ever to get the work done and have all that information in one place.

We hope that this guide has been helpful for you in creating your own digital Classroom.

CPSIA information can be obtained
at www.ICGtesting.com
Printed in the USA
LVHW020336091120
671122LV00008B/340